HAVANESE And HAVANESE DOGS BIBLE

Includes Havanese Puppies, Havanese Dogs, Havanese Breed, Havanese Rescue, Finding Breeders, Havanese Care, Mixes, Bichon Havanese, Havapoo, And More!

By Susanne Saben
© DYM Worldwide Publishers

DYM Worldwide Publishers

ISBN: 978-1-911355-08-3

interpretation of the subject matter herein. Any perceived slights to any specific person(s) or organization(s) are purely unintentional. We have no control over the nature, content, and availability of the websites listed in this book. The inclusion of any website links does not necessarily imply a recommendation or endorse the views expressed within them. DYM Worldwide Publishers takes no responsibility for, and will not be liable for, the websites being temporarily or being removed from the Internet. The accuracy and completeness of the information provided herein and opinions stated herein are not guaranteed or warranted to produce any particular results, and the advice or strategies, contained herein may not be suitable for every individual. The author, publisher, distributors, and/or affiliates shall not be liable for any loss incurred as a consequence of the use and application, directly or indirectly of any information presented in this work. This publication is designed to provide information in regards to the subject matter covered. The information included in this book has been compiled to give an overview of the topics covered. The information contained in this book has been compiled to provide an overview of the subject. It is not intended as medical advice and should not be construed as such. For a firm diagnosis of any medical conditions you should consult a doctor or veterinarian (as related to animal health). The writer, publisher, distributors, and/or affiliates of this work are not responsible for any damages or negative consequences

Foreword

With long silky fur and a friendly personality, the Havanese is by far one of the best dog breeds out there. As the proud owner of a Havanese dog myself, I can attest to the fact that these little dogs are the perfect companion pets. Havanese dogs are energetic and full of life, but they are also very smart and trainable. If you are looking for a new pet, I cannot recommend the Havanese highly enough.

The Havanese is an excellent choice if you are interested in a small-breed dog but there are some things you should know about the Havanese breed before you decide if it is right for you. Having owned my own Havanese for several years, I understand what it takes to keep these dogs happy and healthy – and I am going to share that information with you! By the time you finish this book, you'll know for sure whether a Havanese is the right dog for you and you will be well on your way to becoming the best dog owner you can!

My Havanese, Bailey, has brought endless joy to my life, but he is a little higher maintenance than other dogs I've had in the past. If you want to keep a Havanese puppy or an adult Havanese, you should learn all that you can about these dogs. In this book, you will find a combination of practical information about Havanese dogs as well as plenty of personal anecdotes and tidbits from my years of experience with the breed. So, if you are ready to learn more about the Havanese, just turn the page and keep reading!

Table of Contents

Chapter One: Introduction

Havanese dogs make wonderful pets - keep reading to find out why I love them so much! (and why you will too!)

If you have picked up this book, then I have to assume that you are interested in a fluffy little dog called the Havanese. If so, I want you to know that you are on the right track! I can say from personal experience that there is no better dog breed than the Havanese, and I have worked with many dog breeds in my day, so that is saying something! I am the proud owner of a Havanese myself (his name is Bailey), and I wouldn't give him up for anything in the world!

Some people might say that all fluffy dogs look alike but, to me, the Havanese is a very unique and wonderful breed. Not only are these little dogs smart and energetic, but they are very affectionate with their family, and they love to cuddle. Bailey and I spend most evenings together on the couch, catching up on our favorite TV shows. Havanese dogs are friendly, and they do not have the same tendency to bark at strangers that many small dogs do – this is important to me because I love having friends over! Simply put, if you are looking for a small dog that doesn't have some of the negative small dog characteristics, the Havanese might be right for you.

I know how hard it can be to choose a dog breed, especially when there are so many wonderful options out there. In this book, I hope to provide you with all of the information you need to decide whether or not the Havanese dog is right for you. I will teach you about Havanese temperament and personality as well as the history of the breed and tips for Havanese training. By the time you finish this book, you will have the information you need to decide if the Havanese is a good fit for your family, even if your family is just you. If it is, then you will also have a firm foundation of knowledge to build on, helping you to become the very best Havanese owner that you can be.

So what are you waiting for? Turn the page to keep reading about the beautiful Havanese breed!

Useful Terms to Know

AKC – American Kennel Club, the largest purebred dog registry in the United States

Almond Eye – Referring to an elongated eye shape rather than a rounded shape

Apple Head – A round-shaped skull

Balance – A show term referring to all of the parts of the dog, both moving and standing, which produce a harmonious image

Beard – Long, thick hair on the dog's underjaw

Best in Show – An award is given to the only undefeated dog left standing at the end of judging

Bitch – A female dog

Bite – The position of the upper and lower teeth when the dog's jaws are closed; positions include level, undershot, scissors, or overshot

Blaze – A white stripe running down the center of the face between the eyes

Board – To house, feed, and care for a dog for a fee

Breed – A domestic race of dogs having a common gene pool and characterized appearance/function

Breed Standard – A published document describing the look, movement, and behavior of the perfect specimen of a particular breed

Buff – An off-white to gold coloring

Clip – A method of trimming the coat in some breeds

Coat – The hair covering of a dog; some breeds have two coats, and outer coat and undercoat; also known as a double coat. Examples of breeds with double coats include German Shepherd, Siberian Husky, Akita, etc.

Condition – The health of the dog as shown by its skin, coat, behavior, and general appearance

Crate – A container used to house and transport dogs; also called a cage or kennel

Crossbreed (Hybrid) – A dog having a sire and dam of two different breeds; cannot be registered with the AKC

Dam (bitch) – The female parent of a dog;

Dock – To shorten the tail of a dog by surgically removing the end part of the tail.

Double Coat – Having an outer weather-resistant coat and a soft, waterproof coat for warmth; see above.

Drop Ear – An ear in which the tip of the ear folds over and hangs down; not prick or erect

Entropion – A genetic disorder resulting in the upper or lower eyelid turning in

Fancier – A person who is especially interested in a particular breed or dog sport

Fawn – A red-yellow hue of brown

Feathering – A long fringe of hair on the ears, tail, legs, or body of a dog

Groom – To brush, trim, comb or otherwise make a dog's coat neat in appearance

Heel – To command a dog to stay close by its owner's side

Hip Dysplasia – A condition characterized by the abnormal formation of the hip joint

Inbreeding – The breeding of two closely related dogs of one breed

Kennel – A building or enclosure where dogs are kept

Litter – A group of puppies born at one time

Markings – A contrasting color or pattern on a dog's coat

Mask – Dark shading on the dog's foreface

Mate – To breed a dog and a bitch

Neuter – To castrate a male dog or spay a female dog

Pads – The tough, shock-absorbent skin on the bottom of a dog's foot

Parti-Color – A coloration of a dog's coat consisting of two or more definite, well-broken colors; one of the colors must be white

Pedigree – The written record of a dog's genealogy going back three generations or more

Pied – A coloration on a dog consisting of patches of white and another color

Prick Ear – Ear that is carried erect, usually pointed at the tip of the ear

Puppy – A dog under 12 months of age

Purebred – A dog whose sire and dam belong to the same breed and who are of unmixed descent

Saddle – Colored markings in the shape of a saddle over the back; colors may vary

Shedding – The natural process whereby old hair falls off the dog's body as it is replaced by new hair growth.

Sire – The male parent of a dog

Smooth Coat – Short hair that is close-lying

Spay – The surgery to remove a female dog's ovaries, rendering her incapable of breeding

Trim – To groom a dog's coat by plucking or clipping

Undercoat – The soft, short coat typically concealed by a longer outer coat

Wean – The process through which puppies transition from subsisting on their mother's milk to eating solid food

Whelping – The act of birthing a litter of puppies

Chapter Two: Havanese Dog Overview

Havanese dogs come in all colors and patterns - what kind will you get?

Before you can make an educated decision regarding whether the Havanese is the right choice for you and your family, you need to learn as much as you can about the breed. That is where this book comes in! In this particular chapter, I will introduce you to the Havanese breed, providing you with the basic information you need to know in order to understand what the Havanese is like as a pet. You will also receive valuable information about the different types of Havanese and Havanese mixes as well as the history of the breed.

1.) What is a Havanese Dog or Cuban Dog?

The Havanese dog is a small-breed dog of the Bichon type, and it has been named the national dog of Cuba. This breed was developed from a dog called the Blanquito de la Habana, or the "little white dog of Havana," which is now extinct. Havanese dogs are small in size, but they are fairly sturdy for a small-breed dog – they also have a lively and spirited personality which is part of what makes them so popular as pets.

Havanese dogs are considered to be ideal family pets and great companions because they can adapt well to a variety of living situations and they just love to be with people. Havanese puppies are cuddly little balls of fur that grow into beautiful, thick-coated adults that come in a wide range of colors. The Havanese is a great pet, but it does require a certain degree of care and maintenance, especially if you choose to keep your dog's coat long for show purposes or simply because you like it. However, if you don't mind a little upkeep, and you are looking for a faithful companion, the Havanese might just be the right dog for you.

2.) *Havanese Dog History*

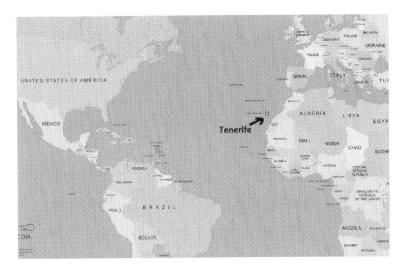

The Bichon Tenerife, originating in the Spanish island of Tenerife is one of the
probable ancestors of the modern-day Havanese.

There is some debate as to the accurate history of the
Havanese breed, but it is known to belong to the Bichon
family of dogs. There are four Bichon-type dogs that all
originated in the Mediterranean area – the Bichon Maltese,
the Bichon Bolognaise, the Bichon Tenerife, and the Bichon
Havanese. All of these breeds were small, primarily white
dogs with cheerful dispositions and they were moved
around the world in the company of sailors. These dogs
became particularly popular on the Canary Island of
Tenerife where they were crossed with other local breeds
until the 14th century when sailors once more discovered
them and brought them back to the continent.

Over the next century or two, the four Bichon breeds were developed independently of one another. The Bichon Tenerife came to be known as the Bichon Frise in 1934 when the breed was admitted into the stud book for the Société Centrale Canine. The breed that came to be referred to as the Maltese was crossed with the Tibetan Terrier and developed for its pure white coat. The Bichon Bolognaise came to be known simply as the Bolognese, and it was developed as a toy breed in Bologna, Italy.

The Bichon Havanese was developed from a number of small, bichon-type dogs that were brought to Cuba by Italian and Spanish sailors. This breed differs from the standard Bichon type in that its coat is not pure white – it exhibits a number of different colors as well as a distinct wave in its fur. This is thought to be the result of crossing the breed with a now-extinct breed of South American poodle, though it may be nothing more than a genetic mutation. Like most Bichon-type dogs, the Havanese is generally left to let its coat grow long.

The Havanese remained a popular breed in Cuba for many years until it was brought to the United States when upper-class Cubans fled to the U.S. during the Cuban Revolution. American breeds immediately took notice of the breed and began to develop it in the states, starting with a gene pool of just 11 dogs. The breed was officially recognized by the American Kennel Club (AKC) in 1996 and, thanks to selective breeding programs, the Havanese is now one of the fastest growing dog breeds in the AKC. In 2013, the breed was ranked 25th according to AKC registration statistics, and it continues to grow in popularity.

3.) *Havanese Weight, Havanese Temperament, and Other Breed Information*

The Havanese is a small-breed dog that is typically classified as a Toy breed. These dogs generally stand between 8 and 12 inches (20 to 30.5 cm) high at maturity and the average Havanese weight is between 7 and 13 pounds (3 to 6 kg). Although the Havanese may be small, it has a relatively sturdy build compared to other toy breeds, and it is a very adaptable breed in terms of living arrangements. Because it is so small, the Havanese breed is a good choice for apartment or condo living, though they can do well in larger homes with big backyards. For the most part, all the Havanese really wants is to spend time with you.

a) Havanese Colors and Coat

In terms of appearance, the Havanese is well known for having a long, wavy coat. The coat is similar in texture to other Bichon-type dogs – it is silky and soft – but it is also very thick and almost curly in some cases. The Havanese coat is also different from other Bichon-type dogs in that it is a double coat but the outer coat is soft, not dense or coarse like some dogs. It is also worth noting that there are many different Havanese colors. While there are white Havanese, there are also black Havanese, brown Havanese, black and white Havanese, and other color combinations. There is no standard color for this breed – they come in all shades of brown, black, tan, cream, white, red, gold, silver, blue, and fawn. Havanese colors may be single, double, or even tri-colored with different types of markings.

Though the color of the Havanese's coat may vary, most dogs of this breed have dark brown eyes lidded with black. Their bodies are sturdy but small with short legs, well-sprung ribs, and a tucked abdomen. The muzzle is full, and it tapers slightly toward a dark nose while the ears are flopped and covered with wavy fur. The tail is carried high over the back, letting its long, feathered fur fall onto the body. The coat grows very long, and trimming is generally not accepted for show dogs except around the feed. Havanese pets, however, can be trimmed.

b) Havanese Personality and Health

In terms of Havanese personality, these are bright and active little dogs. Unlike many small-breed dogs the Havanese is easy to train because they are so smart. They do not have the same tendency to develop a stubborn streak like some smaller dogs. Havanese dogs can, however, be a bit tricky to housebreak so you may need to train them to use a litter box or pad indoors and then transition them into going outside.

The Havanese temperament is very gentle and friendly. These dogs do not tend to bark at strangers, though they can be a little bit shy at first until they are properly introduced. It is important to know that these dogs are very people-oriented, and they need lots of time and daily attention to remain happy and healthy. A Havanese dog that is left alone all day will not be happy, and he may develop problem behavior out of boredom or stress. These dogs can get along with other dogs, but they definitely prefer the company of humans.

Havanese dogs are very adaptable and generally not difficult to care for – your biggest task will probably be Havanese grooming. The Havanese doesn't tend to shed as much as other breeds which leads some to believe that they are hypoallergenic. They do shed, however, but they produce less dander than many dogs which makes them an excellent choice for allergy sufferers. Keep in mind, however, that you will need to brush your dog's coat on an almost-daily basis, and he will need to be professionally groomed and trimmed several times a year as well. This is why some people consider the Havanese breed to be high-maintenance.

In terms of health, the Havanese is actually a very healthy breed – this is somewhat surprising considering the fact that the breed was developed in the U.S. from a gene pool of just 11 dogs. Still, the average Havanese lifespan is between 14 and 16 years, and the breed isn't prone to many serious health problems. The most common health issues that do affect the breed include heart disease, eye problems, tear staining, and some musculoskeletal issues like patellar luxation and hip dysplasia. Responsible breeding practices can help to reduce the risk for these conditions.

c) Summary of Havanese Breed Info

Pedigree: Bichon-type dog, may have been developed from the now-extinct Tenerife dog

AKC Group: Toy Group

Breed Size: small

Height: 8 to 12 inches (20 to 30.5 cm)

Weight: 7 to 13 pounds (3 to 6 kg)

Coat Length: very long

Coat Texture: soft and silky, often wavy; undercoat may or may not be present. Their outer coat is soft and light

Color: white, cream, tan, fawn, red, chocolate, brown, beige, black, silver, blue, etc.

Eyes and Nose: dark brown or black

Ears: flopped ears, well covered in fur

Tail: carried high over the back, feathered fur falls down onto the body

Temperament: friendly, lively, people-oriented, active

Strangers: may be shy around strangers but warms up quickly once introduced

Other Dogs: generally good with other dogs

Other Pets: generally, gets along with other pets

Training: intelligent and very trainable; may take longer to housetrain than larger dogs

Exercise Needs: not overly active or energetic; happy to spend most of its time inside with people

Health Conditions: heart disease, eye problems, tear staining, and some musculoskeletal issues like patellar luxation and hip dysplasia

Lifespan: average 14 to 16 years

4.) *Havanese Types and Mixes*

In recent years there has been a trend toward increased popularity of mixed breeds being referred to as "designer dogs". In many cases, designer dogs are a cross between two pure breeds which makes for an endless list of possibilities. Designer dogs can be developed from any pure breed, but the Havanese is one of the most popular. If you search for Havanese puppies, you will probably come across a number of different Havanese mixes including some of the following:

- Havachon, or Bichon Havanese Mix (Bichon Frise and Havanese)
- Havamalt, or Havanese Maltese Mix (Maltese and Havanese)
- Havashu, or Havanese Shih Tzu Mix (Shih Tzu and Havanese)
- Havapoo, Havanese-Poodle Mix (Havanese and Toy Poodle)

These are just a few of the possible crossings to create a Havanese mix. Each crossbreed has its unique qualities and benefits, but the Havanese Bichon mix is one of the most popular. It is also possible to create a Havanese terrier with any of the various terrier breeds. There are also some size variations of the Havanese dog breed which have come into development recently. These are not separate breeds; they are simply names given to different sizes of Havanese dogs. Tiny Havanese dogs are sometimes called Teacup Havanese or Miniature Havanese. You may also come across a Toy Havanese, though this name is really the same thing since the Havanese is already a toy breed.

If you are thinking about getting a teacup Havanese or a miniature Havanese, you need to be especially careful about where you buy them. Small-breed dogs that are selectively bred to be even smaller than the standard have a higher risk for certain health problems – primarily musculoskeletal issues and dental problems. Spine problems and joint problems are relatively common in miniature and teacup breeds. Plus, dental problems can become a factor since their mouths are so small. Caring for a teacup or miniature Havanese is also tricky because you need to be extra gentle and finding the right amount of food for him to maintain a healthy weight can be difficult as well.

When shopping for Havanese puppies, you may decide that a Havanese mix might be a better choice for you. You can find Havamalt puppies, Havapoo puppies, Bichon Havanese puppies, and other mixes from hobby breeders online. Just be careful to do your research before buying any Havanese mix puppies for sale – you want to make sure that the breeder is knowledgeable and experienced with the breed. Plus, you want to make sure that the dogs used for breeding are in good health and that the proper precautions have been taken to avoid the passing of congenital conditions. Always speak to the breeder directly and take a look at the puppies available before you put down a deposit.

Havanese Mix Pictures

When you cross two purebred dogs to create a mixed breed or designer dog, it's hard to predict exactly what the dog will look like or act like – this is the case for Havanese mixes just as much as it is for any of the many dog breeds out there. Each Havanese mix is unique depending on the second breed used in the crossing – this will determine details such as the dog's size, appearance, coat, and temperament. Just like the Havanese breed itself, Havanese mixes can make wonderful pets for the right family as long as you do your research beforehand to ensure that it will be a good fit for you and yours.

To help give you an idea what these dogs might look like, I have provided you with some photos of different Havanese mixed breed dogs:

Havachon (Bichon Frise and Havanese) Bichon Havanese Mix

The wavy fur of the Bichon Frise and the friendly temperament of the Havanese!

Havamalt (Maltese and Havanese) Havanese Maltese Mix

Fluffy, cute, and cuddly - what more could you ask for?

Havashu (Shih Tzu and Havanese) Havanese Shih Tzu Mix

Look at that long, lovely coat - better keep a brush handy!

Havapoo (Havanese and Toy Poodle) Havanese Poodle Mix

How could you possibly say No to that adorable face?

Chapter Three: Havanese Costs and Other Practical Havanese Tips

When it comes to your daily walk, will you take charge or will your Havanese be the one walking you?

Now that you have a better understanding of the Havanese dog breed you may have a good idea whether it is the right breed for you. Before you decide, however, I would encourage you to learn some of the practical aspects of keeping Havanese dogs as pets. In this chapter, I will provide you with valuable information about licensing your dog, keeping more than one Havanese, keeping Havanese dogs with other pets, and the costs associated with these

dogs. You will also receive a list of pros and cons for the
breed to consider.

1.) Do You Need a License for an Adult Havanese?

Whether you are buying a dog or some other kind of pet, it is always a good idea to check your regional or local requirements for licensing and permits. The licensing requirements for pets including dogs are different in the various countries, and even in different states. Even if your state doesn't mandate that you have to license your Havanese, it might still be a good idea. When you license your dog, he will be assigned a specific license number that will be associated with your contact information – if he gets lost and someone finds him, he or she may be able to contact you using the information from the license.

There are no federal licensing requirements for dogs in the United States – these things are determined instead at the state level. Most states do require dog owners to license their dogs, and the licenses are generally renewable annually. Dog licenses in the United States only cost about $25 (£22.50), and they must be paired with an updated rabies vaccination – each year you will have to renew the license and prove that your dog is current on his rabies vaccine as well.

The licensing requirements for dogs in the United Kingdom and in other parts of Europe are a little bit different. The

United Kingdom makes it mandatory for all dog owners to license their dogs and the cost is similar to the expense of a dog license in the U.S. One major difference you should keep in mind is that dogs in the U.K. do not need to be vaccinated against rabies because the virus has been eradicated in the U.K. If you plan to move your dog into or out of the country, however, you will need to obtain an Animal Movement License (AML) to make sure your dog doesn't contract or spread any diseases during his travel.

2.) How Many Havanese Dogs Should You Get?

Wetter is better! Havanese dogs love to swim!

Many people wonder whether it is better to keep one
Havanese on his own or to get two dogs. The Havanese
breed is compatible with other dogs, but there are some
things you should think about. Toy breeds do not always
get along with large dogs unless they have a very calm and
gentle temperament. You also need to remember that
Havanese dogs are very people-oriented – they prefer the
company of humans to that of other dogs. Still, if you must
leave your dog alone for extended periods of time, it may
help for him to have a canine companion.

3.) Do Havanese Dogs Get Along with Other Pets?

Because the Havanese dog breed was developed solely as a companion pet, you shouldn't have to worry about your dog having a strong prey drive. Most Havanese dogs get along well with cats and other pets, especially if they are raised together from a young age. If you want to make sure that your dog gets along with everyone in your house, you should start your Havanese puppy with socialization and training as early as possible – the first three months are particularly critical for this. You should also be sure to supervise your dog when he interacts with other pets, in particular for the first few times, to make sure that nothing happens to either of them.

4.) Havanese Dog Price and Costs

*Catch me if you can! Just try to wrestle your Havanese's favorite toy away
from him.*

Before you decide whether or not to buy a Havanese dog,
you need to make sure that you can cover the costs of dog
ownership. Not only do you need to think about the
average cost of Havanese puppies for sale, but you also
need to think about recurring monthly costs for food and
veterinary care. In this section, you will receive an overview
of the initial costs of owning a Havanese as well as the
recurring monthly costs of Havanese ownership.

a. Price of a Havanese Dog for Sale and Other Initial Costs

The initial costs for keeping a Havanese dog include the price to purchase the dog, the cost of a crate and/or dog bed, food and water bowls, toys and accessories, microchipping, vaccinations, spay/neuter surgery, and grooming supplies. <u>You will find an overview of each of these costs as well as an estimate for each cost below</u>:

Havanese Dog Price – The main cost you will have to cover is the actual price for the dog. The average price Havanese puppy breeders charge can vary widely depending on a number of factors. Purebred Havanese puppies are more expensive than mixes and show-quality puppies are most costly than pet-quality puppies. The average Havanese price for a pet-quality puppy is between $1,000 and $1,500 (£691 - £1,037) while a show-quality dog might cost between $2,000 and $3,000 (£1,382 - £2,074). If you chose to get your dog from a Havanese dog rescue, the cost of Havanese adoption is usually under $300 (£207).

Crate and/or Dog Bed – When you start training your Havanese you will want to have a crate that you can keep him in overnight and when you are away from home. To make your dog's crate more comfortable, you should line it with a blanket or dog bed. The average cost for these things together is around $50 (£34.50).

Food/Water Bowls – Buying quality food and water bowls for your Havanese is important because he will use them every day. Your best option is stainless steel because it is easy to clean and doesn't harbor bacteria – ceramic is another good choice. The average costs for a quality set of stainless steel bowls are about $20 (£13.80).

Toys and Accessories – In addition to food and water bowls, your Havanese will also need certain accessories like chew toys, a collar, a leash, and perhaps a harness. The cost for these items varies depending on quality, but you should budget about $50 (£34.50) for all of these costs combined.

Microchipping – Having your Havanese microchipped is not a requirement, but it is an excellent idea. A microchip is similar to a license in that it comes with a number that is correlated with your contact information. The difference is that the microchip is implanted under your dog's skin so it cannot be lost. The procedure only takes a few minutes, and it doesn't hurt your dog – plus, it only costs about $30 (£20.75) if you go to a clinic or shelter.

Vaccinations – Immediately after Havanese puppies are born they drink their mother's milk which contains antibodies to protect them until their immune systems develop. During the first year, you will also need to make sure your Havanese puppy gets certain vaccines to protect him against disease. Depending what Havanese breeder you get your puppy from, he may already have one or more vaccinations under his belt. Still, you should budget a cost of about $50 (£34.50) for initial vaccinations to be safe.

Spay/Neuter Surgery – If you do not plan to breed your Havanese (and you should think carefully before you do), you should have your dog altered before 6 months of age. If you go to a veterinary surgeon, this procedure could cost you hundreds of dollars, but you can save money by going to a vet clinic. The average clinic cost for spay surgery is $100 to $200 (£69 - £138), and the average cost for neuter surgery is around $50 to $100 (£34.50 - £69).

Grooming Supplies – To keep your Havanese dog's coat healthy and tangle-free, you'll need to brush and comb it several times a week – you may also want to trim the fur between your dog's toes once a week. For grooming supplies you will need a wide-toothed comb, a wire-pin brush, some dog shampoo, and a set of nail clippers – if you want to trim your dog's fur at home, you might also need a trimmer. The cost for these supplies varies depending on quality, but you should set aside $50 (£34.50) to be safe.

To put all of this information together in your head, here is a chart detailing the costs for one Havanese and for two Havanese dogs as well as a total cost at the end:

Initial Costs for Havanese Dogs		
Cost	**One Dog**	**Two Dogs**
Havanese Price	$300 to $3,000 (£207 - £2,074)	$600 to $6,000 (£415 - £4,148)
Crate/Bed	$50 (£34.50)	$100 (£69)
Food/Water Bowls	$20 (£13.80)	$40 (£27.65)
Toys/Accessories	$50 (£34.50)	$100 (£69)
Microchipping	$30 (£20.75)	$60 (£41.50)
Vaccinations	$50 (£34.50)	$100 (£69)

Spay/Neuter	$50 to $200	$100 to $400
	(£34.50 - £138)	(£69 - £277)
Grooming Supplies	$50 (£34.50)	$50 (£34.50)
Total	$600 to $3,450	$1,150 to $6,850
	(£415 – £2,385)	(£795 – £4,736)

*Prices may vary by region and are subject to change.

**Prices are calculated based on the exchange rate of $1 = £0.69

b. Monthly Costs for a Full Grown Havanese

The monthly costs for keeping a Havanese as a pet include all of the recurring costs you need to cover on a monthly or yearly basis. These costs may include the cost of food and treats, veterinary care, license renewal, grooming costs, and others. You will find an overview of each of these expenses as well as an estimate for each cost below:

Food and Treats – Because the Havanese is a toy breed, your monthly costs for food shouldn't be very high. You can expect to spend about $30 (£20.75) on a large bag of high-quality dog food that will last you about a month.

Veterinary Care – Once your Havanese puppy gets all the shots he needs during his first year, you will only need to take him to the vet once or twice a year for check-ups. The average cost for a vet check-up is about $40 (£27.65). If you have two vet visits per year and divide that total cost over 12 months, you will get a monthly cost around $7 (£4,80).

License Renewal – Renewing your Havanese dog's license each year will not be a major expense – it should only cost you about $25 (£17.30). If you divide that cost over twelve months, you are left with a monthly cost of just $2 (£1.40).

Grooming – One of your biggest monthly costs for your dog is going to be Havanese grooming. You'll need to brush your dog's coat several times a week yourself but should also have your dog professionally groomed several times per year; most owners recommend grooming every 3 months. If you don't plan to show your Havanese, you may also want to have his coat trimmed short. The average cost for Havanese grooming is about $50 (£34.50) and four visits per year divided over twelve months is a monthly cost around $17 (£11.75).

Other Costs – In addition to the costs that have already been mentioned, you may find yourself dealing with unexpected costs for the replacement of toys and food bowls, or you might need to replace your dog's collar. These costs will not occur every month, but you should set aside about $10 (£6.90) each month to be prepared.

To put all of this information together in your head, here is a chart detailing the costs for one Havanese and for two Havanese dogs as well as a total cost at the end:

Monthly Costs for Havanese Dogs		
Cost	**One Dog**	**Two Dogs**
Food and Treats	$30 (£20.75)	$60 (£41.50)
Vet Care	$7 (£4.80)	$14 (£9.70)
License Renewal	$2 (£1.40)	$4 (£2.75)
Grooming	$17 (£11.75)	$34 (£23.50)
Other Costs	$10 (£6.90)	$20 (£13.80)
Total	$66 (£46)	$132 (£91)

*Prices may vary by region and are subject to change.
**Prices are calculated based on the exchange rate of $1 = £0.69

5.) *Havanese Dog Pros and Cons*

Every dog breed has its own unique appearance and personality traits – some are good, some are bad. Before you decide to get a Havanese, you should take the time to learn about the pros and cons for the breed. This will help to ensure that you really know what you are getting into with these dogs. You will find a list of pros and cons below:

Pros for the Havanese Dog

- Very small in size, makes an excellent choice for apartment or condo life but can adapt to other living situations
- Naturally friendly and even-tempered breed
- Very people-oriented, forms strong bonds with family and is great with singles as well
- Generally, a very healthy breed with a long lifespan between 14 and 16 years
- Attractive breed, comes in a wide variety of colors and straight or wavy fur
- Not an overly active breed, doesn't require a great deal of daily exercise
- Generally, doesn't bark very much; shy around strangers but warms up quickly

- Smart and trainable, especially if you start while the dog is very young

Cons for the Havanese Dog

- Should not be left alone for extended periods of time; may not be a good choice for busy singles/families
- Long, wavy coat requires lots of grooming and maintenance to stay healthy
- May be tricky to housetrain (like most toy breeds), may need to start with pads and transition to outside
- Unlikely to make a good watch dog (doesn't bark at strangers)
- May be expensive to purchase, especially for a purebred, show-quality dog

Chapter Four: Havanese Puppies and Where to Find Havanese Puppies for Sale

They may be cute and fluffy, but Havanese puppies can be a lot of work!

If you have decided that the Havanese is the right breed for you, your next step is to learn where to find one! There is nothing that can compare to the joy of bringing home a new Havanese puppy, but raising a puppy can be a challenge. If you aren't sure that you want to deal with the "puppy phase" you may want to think about adopting from a Havanese rescue. In this chapter, you will learn about where to find Havanese dogs for sale from Havanese breeders as well as information about finding a rescue dog. You will also receive tips for picking out a healthy puppy from your choice of Havanese breeders.

1.) Where to Find Havanese Breeders with Havanese Dogs for Sale

If you are like many of the new dog owners I meet, your first instinct when you are looking for a Havanese puppy is to go to the pet store. While you may be able to find a Havanese puppy for sale at your local pet store, you need to think carefully about whether that is really the best option. While the puppies you see in the pet store are undeniably adorable, and they might look like they are in good health, there is really no way to tell. Do you really want to take the risk of potentially bringing home a puppy that is carrying some kind of disease?

What most people do not realize is that many pet stores get their puppies from puppy mills. A puppy mill is a breeding operation that puts profit over the welfare of the dogs. They force dogs to reproduce litter after litter with minimal veterinary care, keeping them in squalid conditions. Puppy mills do not screen their breeding stock to minimize the risk of passing on genetic conditions which means that the puppies have an increased likelihood of inheriting those conditions. When you buy a puppy from a pet store, the store may not tell you exactly where the puppy came from, and you may not receive any papers showing his pedigree and providing information about the parents.

If you want to make sure that the Havanese puppies for sale are healthy and well-bred, your best bet is to find a Havanese breeder. The simplest way to find a breeder is to perform an online search. You may also be able to find information about local breeders at the pet store or at your local veterinary office or clinic. Do not just buy a puppy from the first breeder you find, however. You need to screen the breeders to ensure that they are responsible and experienced – you want to make sure that the puppy you end up buying is of the highest quality possible.

In order to ensure that you pick a responsible Havanese breeder, follow the steps below:

- Gather information about several Havanese breeders using whatever methods you have available to you.
- Take the time to visit the website for each breeder.
  - Look for relevant information like AKC or Kennel Club membership as well as affiliations with local or regional breed clubs.
  - Read the information provided on the website about the breeder to help determine whether they are a legitimate operation or just a backyard breeder.
  - Look for red flags like extremely high Havanese prices, lack of breed club registration, no information about the breeding stock, etc.

- Narrow down your list of breeders, eliminating any that seem to be irresponsible or hobby breeders based on your review of their websites.
- Contact the remaining breeders on your list and schedule a face-to-face interview, is possible.
  - Ask the breeder detailed questions about the breeding operation including his experience with dog breeding in general and with the dog breed Havanese in particular.
  - Ask about the pedigree and health status of the breeding stock for whatever litters are available – it is a red flag if the breeder won't give you this information.
  - Ask about the policy for reserving a puppy – a reputable breeder won't let you purchase a puppy outright without meeting you, and he will be just as eager to ask you questions as you are to ask him in order to ensure that you will give the puppy a good home.
- After speaking to the breeders over the phone or in person, ask for a tour of the breeding facilities.
  - Make sure to view the facilities where the breeding stock is kept, in addition to where the puppies are being kept.

- o Ensure that the facilities are clean and well-kept – if the place is dirty or if there are signs of diarrhea, avoid purchasing from that breeder.
- o Make sure that the breeding stock is in good health and that the dogs are a good example of the breed standard – view the pedigrees and health certificates for the dogs, if possible.
- o Consider it a red flag if the breeder is not willing to show you the facilities and the breeding stock.

Once you've narrowed down your list of breeders, you can start looking at and interacting with the puppies that are currently available. You will find detailed information for picking out a healthy Havanese puppy in the next section.

a) Finding Teacup Havanese or Toy Havanese

If you are looking for a Teacup Havanese or a Toy Havanese, be very careful about which breeder you choose. Remember that a Toy Havanese is no different from a regular Havanese because these dogs are already a toy breed. If you want a Havanese that is bred small, a Teacup Havanese may be what you want. You can find breeders for Teacup Havanese puppies the same way you would find a

normal Havanese breeder – just be sure to ask plenty of
questions to ensure that the breeder is reputable.

b) Finding a Havanese Terrier, Havamalt Puppies or Havapoo Puppies

When shopping for a Havanese Terrier, Havamalt puppies,
or Havapoo puppies, do not fall prey to the temptation to
buy the first puppy you see. It is important to remember
that crossbreed dogs like Havanese mixes can inherit any
combination of traits from their parents, so you want to
choose a puppy that is bred from two quality specimens of
the parent breeds. You also need to be wary of backyard
breeders that may charge extremely high prices for what is
essentially a crossbreed dog.

2.) *How to Choose a Healthy Havanese Puppy*

*If you want to check your Havanese puppy for signs of good health
you will have to catch him first!*

Once you've narrowed down your list of breeders and have chosen one or two you consider to be the best, actually take the time to view the litters of puppies available. You want to interact with the puppies to make sure that they have the right Havanese temperament, and you want to examine them to ensure that they are healthy.

On the following pages you will find a list of steps to follow in picking out a healthy Havanese for sale from a breeder:

- Before you do anything else, observe the puppies to see how they interact with each other – make sure that they are active and playful, not lethargic or depressed.
- Gauge the response of the puppies to your presence – they may be a little wary around strangers, but they should not be overly frightened. They should get over their nervousness quickly and show curiosity about you.
- Kneel down and let the puppies approach you – interact with them a little bit by petting them gently and speaking to them, making sure that they have a positive response.
- Pick up the puppies one by one to gauge their temperaments and to check for physical signs of illness or injury.
- Examine the puppies one-by-one to make sure they are in good health and condition. A healthy puppy will display the following:
  o Clear, bright eyes with no sign of discharge.
  o Clean ears – no redness, swelling, or odor.
  o No sign of diarrhea under the tail.
  o Clean, soft fur with no patches missing, even in texture.
  o No bumps or wounds on the body.
  o Healthy activity and sound movement.

- Ask the breeder for the vet and medical information for whatever puppy you are considering to confirm that it is in good health.
- If you strike a bond with one of the puppies and are able to determine that it is in good health, you can ask the breeder about the process of putting down a deposit.

Keep in mind that puppies should not be separated from their mother until they are completely weaned – this usually happens by the time they are 8 weeks old. A responsible breeder will never separate the puppies before this age, and they will most certainly not send a puppy home that is younger than 8 weeks.

3.) *Havanese Rescue and Finding Havanese Puppies for Adoption*

Raising a Havanese puppy can be a big challenge, especially if you are a new dog owner. Not only do you have to go through the process of socializing your puppy but you also have to worry about housebreaking and obedience training. For some people, that is simply too much work. If you find yourself in this boat, you may want to consider a rescue Havanese.

Rescue dogs have many benefits. By adopting a dog, you are effectively saving a life – you will also be doing your part by not supporting pet store puppy mills. Another benefit of adopting a dog is that the dog will likely already be housetrained and may have some obedience training under his belt as well. One benefit that many people do not consider is the fact that the personality of a puppy can change as he matures – if you adopt an adult Havanese, his personality will already be mostly set so you can determine whether the two of you are a good match.

If you still have your heart set on a puppy but you like the idea of rescue dogs, you may be able to find Havanese puppies for adoption. Check your local animal shelter or rescue league and see if you can put your name on a

waiting list so the shelter will contact you if Havanese
puppies become available. Another option is to find and
work with a dedicated Havanese rescue. To help you out,
you will find a list of rescues that may have Havanese dogs
for adoption in the U.S. and the U.K.:

United States Havanese Dog Rescues

Havanese Rescue, Inc. http://havaneserescue.com/

Havanese Angel League Organization.
http://www.rescuedhavanese.org/

The Havanese Club of America, Inc.
http://www.havanese.org/rescue

You can also find local animal shelters and rescues in your
area by using these directories:

**American Society for the Prevention of Cruelty to
Animals (ASPCA).** http://www.aspca.org/

Pet Finder Animal Shelters & Rescues.

https://www.petfinder.com/animal-shelters-and-rescues/

United Kingdom Havanese Dog Rescues

Havanese – Netherlands Dog Rescue.

http://www.netherlandsdogrescue.co.uk/

The Havanese Club of Great Britain.

http://havaneseclub.co.uk/

Small Dog Rescue. http://www.smalldogrescue.co.uk/

The Little Dog Rescue. http://www.littledogrescue.co.uk/

Little Black Dog Rescue.

http://www.littleblackdogrescue.org/

Chapter Five: Havanese Dog Care Guide

On a hot summer's day, your Havanese will appreciate a dip in the stream to cool off!

Once you bring your Havanese dog home, it becomes your job to take care of him. Not only will you need to provide for your dog's habitat requirements, but you also need of fulfill his needs for exercise and provide him with a healthy diet. In this chapter, you will receive an overview of information about the home requirements for Havanese dogs. You will also receive a detailed overview of the nutritional demands of the breed as well as tips for choosing a quality dog food diet. Finally, you will also learn about the grooming needs of the Havanese.

1.) Havanese Home Requirements

Although the Havanese is a lively and playful little dog, you will find that the breed doesn't need an excessive amount of exercise. In fact, I can tell you from experience that many Havanese dogs are perfectly happy to be couch potatoes, napping all day except for when it is time to eat or time to play. To make sure that your Havanese has the opportunity to work off any extra energy, however, you should plan to take your dog for a 20- to 30-minute walk once per day.

Not only does the Havanese have low exercise requirements, but these dogs also do not require a lot of space – they are perfectly happy in an apartment or condo building. All they really want is to spend time with you. Though physical exercise is not a major concern for Havanese dogs, you do need to think about mental stimulation. These dogs are very smart, and they can develop problem behaviors if they get bored. The Havanese is not a breed that does well when left alone for extended periods of time.

To make sure your dog gets the mental stimulation he needs, consider purchasing him a wide assortment of different toys. Buying your dog a variety of toys will give him the chance to try them out and to decide which ones he likes best. Be sure to include plenty of chew toys (especially while your Havanese is still a puppy) and don't forget to include some interactive or puzzle toys. Kong toys are an excellent example of an interactive toy – you can fill them with peanut butter, or small treats and your dog will spend hours playing with it, trying to get the treats. If you are worried about your dog getting bored or lonely while you are away, leave him with an interactive toy.

Something else you should consider in regard to your dog's home requirements is setting up a special area of the house that your dog can call his own. It is highly recommended that you have a crate for your Havanese – you will use it for crate training – but you should also have a larger area set up where you can put him while you can't keep an eye on him but you don't necessarily want to confine him to the crate. This is where a puppy playpen comes in handy – you can enclose the area surrounding your dog's crate to give him some free space while limiting the amount of trouble he can get into. If you have a small spare room in your house that you can close off with a baby gate, that is a good option as well.

To set up your Havanese dog's special area, start with a crate and line it with a comfy blanket or dog bed. Your dog's crate should only be large enough for him to stand up, sit down, turn around, and lie down in comfortably – you do not want too much extra space. This is vital for crate training because you want your dog to view the crate as his "den" – dogs have a natural aversion to soiling their dens. If the crate is too large, it increases the risk that your dog will have an accident when he is in it.

In addition to providing your dog with a crate in his special area, you should also place your dog's food and water bowls here, as well as his treats. Some people prefer to feed their dogs in the kitchen, but I personally think that my Havanese likes having his own little space where he can eat, sleep, and play. If you choose to feed your dog in the kitchen, you should still provide him with a water bowl in his area. Stainless steel bowls are my preference because they are lightweight and easy to clean, plus they do not harbor bacteria like plastic does when it becomes scratched.

2.) *Havanese Dog Feeding Guide*

Yum yum yum! What will you feed your Havanese?

The diet you feed your Havanese is extremely important – it will play a major role in determining his long-term health and wellness. I have seen many dog owners make the mistake of just picking a bag of dog food off the pet store shelves without even reading the label. I am ashamed to admit that I used to do this too until I learned the basics about dog nutrition and actually made an effort to understand them. Once you learn about your dog's nutritional needs, you will understand the importance of feeding him a healthy diet. That is what you will learn in this section.

a.) Nutritional Needs for Havanese Dogs

Like all living things, dogs require a balance of protein, fat, and carbohydrate in their diet as well as water and certain vitamins and minerals. Humans need the same nutrients, but in different ratios – that is why you can't just set a place for your dog at the dinner table. The most important thing you need to know about the nutritional requirements for dogs is that they are primarily carnivores – this means that the majority of their nutrition needs to come from animal products, not plant products.

For dogs, protein is the most important nutritional consideration – it provides your dog with amino acids which are the building blocks of healthy muscle and tissue. There are twenty-two different amino acids, and your Havanese dog's body is capable of synthesizing (producing) twelve of them. The remaining ten amino acids are called essential amino acids because they must come from the dog's diet. Animal proteins like fresh meat are considered complete protein sources because they contain all ten of these essential amino acids. Some plant products that contain protein, but they are less biologically valuable for your dog than animal proteins.

Next to protein, fat is the next most important nutritional consideration for dogs because it is the most concentrated source of energy available to dogs. Though you may have been conditioned to think that all fats are bad, they are actually excellent for dogs as long as they come from natural animal sources. Chicken fat, for example, might sound gross to you but it is a valuable ingredient in dog food – fish oils like salmon oil, or menhaden oil are also valuable additions.

Your Havanese dog's body has evolved to derive the majority of its nutrition from protein and fat, but it is still capable of processing a limited amount of carbohydrate. Carbohydrates provide your dog with dietary fiber to support healthy digestion, and they also contain some essential vitamins and minerals. Dogs have a limited ability to digest high-fiber foods, however, so the carbohydrates in your dog's diet need to come from digestible sources, primarily cooked whole grains like brown rice and oatmeal as well as gluten-free alternatives like potatoes, peas, and sweet potatoes.

Now that you have a basic understanding of the different components of a dog's diet you may be wondering about how much of each of these nutrients your dog really needs. Puppies have very high requirements for protein because their bodies are still growing and developing – the minimum amount of your Havanese puppy's diet that should come from protein is 22%. For adult dogs, the minimum protein requirement is 18%, but the more protein your dog gets, the better (as long as it comes from quality animal sources). For fat, the minimum requirement for puppies is 8%, and the minimum for adults is 5%.

These numbers are minimums – the actual amount that your dog should be getting could be much higher. For puppies, the recommended range for protein is really between 22% and 32% and fat is 10% to 25%. For adult dogs, ideal protein levels are closer to 30% and fat levels are up to 20%. Active and working dogs may have higher needs for both protein and fat, but the Havanese is not considered a working breed. The only time your Havanese might need more than the stated amounts of protein and fat is if she becomes pregnant – then she needs a minimum of 20% fat and 25% to 35% protein.

b.) Choosing a Healthy Dog Food

To ensure that your Havanese dog gets the nutrition he needs, you need to choose a high-quality dog food to feed him. Unfortunately, many people do not realize that not all dog foods are created equal, and the worst thing you can do is shop by price. The fact of the matter is that the cheapest dog foods are also the lowest quality – if you want your dog to get a healthy diet, you will need to spend a little bit more.

To give you an idea, a large bag of low-quality dog food might cost about $15. For a large bag of a high-quality, all-natural dog food you could spend as much as $50 (€44.50). Before you get too worried, remember that there are options in between these two spectrums. You can still find a quality dog food made with real ingredients in the $30 (€26.70) range and feel good that your dog is getting the nutrients he needs. If you feed him a low-quality diet, you may end up spending more in the long run for vet bills because he may develop nutritional deficiencies or other problems.

When shopping for dog food, there are three things you should look for on the label. The first is the AAFCO statement of nutritional adequacy. The American Association of Feed Control Officials (AAFCO) is responsible for regulating the manufacture and sale of pet food and animal feeds. This organization has established profiles for the minimum nutritional requirements for dogs and cats in different life stages. They evaluate commercial pet food products, comparing them to those profiles, to determine if they are complete and balanced for the intended animal. If the product meets those requirements the package will have some sort of statement on it that looks something like this:

"[Product] is formulated to meet the nutritional levels established by the AAFCO Dog Food nutrient profiles for [Life Stage]."

If the dog food product you are looking at carries this statement you can rest assured that it will at least meet the basic nutritional needs for your Havanese. In the United Kingdom, pet food regulation is based on the Feeding Stuffs Act – all ingredients used in pet food must be fit for human consumption. All products that are fit for daily consumption must be labeled "Complete Feedingstuff" or "Complete Petfood" while foods designed for intermittent feeding are labeled "Complementary Feedingstuff" or "Complementary Petfood".

After checking for these statements, you should take a look at the Guaranteed Analysis. This is the part of the label that tells you how much crude protein, crude fat, and crude fiber the product contains – it also tells you how much moisture is in it. You can compare these values to the minimum requirements from the last section to make sure that they are within the proper range. This is an excellent tool to use in comparing different dog food products.

The final thing you need to look at on the product label is the ingredients list. The ingredients list on a dog food package is organized in descending order by volume – the ingredients at the top of the list are used in the highest quantity. When you read the ingredients list, you want to see high-quality ingredients throughout, but you want to see a quality protein source at the very top. Fresh meats like chicken, turkey, lamb, and fish are good protein sources for dogs like the Havanese. Do not freak out if you see the word "meal" attached, either. Meat meals are already cooked to a moisture level around 10%, so they are a much more concentrated source of protein than fresh meats which contain as much as 80% moisture.

In addition to quality proteins, you also want to see animal fats and digestible carbohydrates on the list. It is okay if the product has more than one carbohydrate as long as they are both quality sources, but be wary of any product that has more than two or three carbohydrates – especially if they come from corn, wheat, or soy ingredients which have limited nutritional value for dogs. You also want to avoid products that have a lot of plant proteins like pea protein, potato protein, or alfalfa meal. Low-quality manufacturers sometimes use these ingredients to increase the protein content of their foods without actually adding more meat.

Not only should you pay attention to the ingredients that ARE included in the list, but you should also make note of the things that AREN'T there. Avoid products made with artificial additives like colors, flavors, and preservatives. You should also avoid products made with by-products and low-quality fillers. If the list is full of unidentifiable ingredients or things that sound like chemicals, it probably isn't a quality product. You want to see plenty of fresh meats, animal fats, digestible carbohydrates, and fruits and vegetables on the list.

Some other beneficial additives for high-quality dog foods yes include prebiotics, probiotics, and chelated minerals. Many quality dog foods use dried fermentation products in their recipes – these act as probiotics, helping to support your Havanese's digestive system. Chelated minerals are simply minerals that have been chemically bonded to protein molecules – this makes them easier for your dog's body to digest and absorb. Vitamin supplements can also be beneficial, but it is always better to see natural sources of vitamins and minerals like fresh fruits and vegetables instead of synthetic supplements.

When shopping for a commercial dog food for your Havanese, keep all of this information in mind. Use the details provided on the product label to compare your options. If there is no AAFCO statement or if the ✓ yes Guaranteed Analysis doesn't show the right ratios, avoid the product. If you have two products that seem to be nutritionally balanced, then compare the ingredients lists to choose the better option.

c.) Tips for Feeding Havanese Dogs

While all dogs have the same basic nutritional needs, there are some differences in the dietary requirements for small-breed dogs like the Havanese. Because these dogs are so small, you might assume that they do not need a lot of food. While the actual volume of food a Havanese eats is much smaller than the amount of food a Great Dane would eat, you might be surprised to learn that small dogs actually need more calories per pound than large dogs.

Consider the fact that an 110-pound (50 kg) Great Dane needs an average of 2,500 calories per day. If you divide it up, you will find that the Great Dane needs about 23 calories per pound of bodyweight. A Havanese adult dog, on the other hand, might weigh 11 pounds (5 kg) and need just 450 calories per day. If you do the math, you will see that the Havanese needs about 41 calories per pound of bodyweight. Does this surprise you?

The reason small-breed dogs need so many calories is because they have such a fast metabolism. The faster the dog's metabolism, the more energy he needs during the day to support it and that energy comes in the form of calories from food. Small-breed dogs like the Havanese need higher levels of fat in particular since fat is the most highly concentrated source of energy, containing 9 calories per gram as opposed to 4 calories per gram for protein and carbohydrates.

To make sure that your Havanese gets the calories he needs, you should choose a high-quality commercial dog food that is formulated for small-breed dogs and follow the feeding recommendations on the package. It is important to remember that these recommendations are just that – recommendations – you may need to make adjustments. Start by feeding your dog the recommended daily amount and monitor his weight and activity for a few weeks. If your Havanese gains too much weight you can reduce his daily portion – if he loses weight or appears to be lacking energy, increase his portion.

While some people feed their dogs just once or twice a day, I personally feed my Havanese three small meals a day. By breaking up my dog's daily portion into three smaller meals, I am making sure that he gets a steady stream of energy throughout the day to support his fast metabolism. Smaller dogs have small stomachs, also, so they are physically incapable of eating very large meals anyway. It is up to you to decide how to feed your Havanese, but now that you know a bit more about his nutritional and calorie needs you can make an informed decision.

3.) Havanese Shedding and Grooming Requirements

Look at all that hair! Brush your Havanese often to control shedding.

In addition to providing your dog with a space to call his own and a healthy diet, you also need to take care of his coat. The Havanese may be small, but he has a thick coat that grows very long. Surprisingly, Havanese dogs do not shed a great deal – this makes them an excellent choice for allergy sufferers – but they are not completely hypoallergenic (no dog is). Though Havanese shedding is not a big concern, you still need to brush your dog's coat daily and make sure he gets groomed when needed.

The frequency with which you have your dog groomed will depend on whether you are keeping him strictly as a pet or if you plan to show him. The Havanese breed standard prohibits trimming and sculpting of the coat except for the hair on the feet and in the genital area. You can, however, cord the coat. Cording your Havanese dog's coat involves separating the coat into dreadlocks – this type of coat takes a long time to develop, and it requires a good deal of maintenance as well.

If you are keeping your dog just as a pet, you have the freedom to trim his coat as you like. I am personally a fan of the puppy cut because it is the easiest to maintain. With a puppy cut, you trim the fur on the body and legs to a length between 1 and 3 inches (2.5 to 7.6 cm) while leaving the hair on the head, ears, and tail a little longer to preserve the characteristic Havanese appearance. A pet clip may involve leaving the hair a little bit longer but shaping it to make brushing and grooming easier.

You should plan to brush your Havanese's coat on a daily or near-daily basis to prevent mats and tangles. You should also have him professionally groomed every 6 to 8 weeks. In terms of bathing, you want to avoid doing it too often because it can dry out your dog's skin and lead to irritation. Because the Havanese's coat is so thick and long, however, it tends to gather dirt and dust easily. Bathe your dog as needed but try not to do it any more frequently than every two weeks or so.

a. Brushing and Bathing

Brushing your dog's coat several times a week is very important. Not only does it help to remove dead hair before it can form a mat in your dog's coat, but it also helps to distribute the natural oils from his skin to keep his coat smooth and shiny. The best grooming tools to have on hand for your Havanese include a small slicker brush, a wire-pin brush, a wide-toothed comb, and a flea comb. I would also personally recommend that you have a bottle of spray conditioner as well – it will be very helpful if you have to deal with a lot of tangles or mats.

To brush your Havanese, start by spritzing his coat lightly with the spray conditioner. Have your dog lay on his side then use the wire-pin brush to brush the legs on that side. Start near the feet, brushing down toward the toes in the direction of hair growth and slowly work your way up the leg, starting a little higher with each pass. After finishing the legs, work your way up the body until you reach the backbone. At this point, you can turn your dog over and repeat the process on the other side. When finished, have your dog roll onto his back so you can brush his chest and the underside of his body.

While brushing your dog's coat, you need to work slowly and carefully to avoid hurting him if you encounter a snag or a mat. If you find a tangle, try to pull it apart gently by hand or use the wide-toothed comb to work through it. If you absolutely must cut it out, pinch the hair at the base of the mat between the mat and your dog's skin then cut a few hairs at a time, gently pulling the mat until it comes free. This will help to keep you from accidentally cutting your dog's skin. You can use the fine end of the comb to brush the hair on your dog's face and ears.

If you need to bathe your Havanese, you can do so after you are finished brushing him; brushing your dog before a bath will help to get rid of dead hair so you can work the soap into the coat more thoroughly. Fill your bathtub with just a few inches of lukewarm water then place your dog in it. Use a cup or a hand sprayer to wet down your dog's coat then use a little bit of dog-friendly shampoo and work it into a thick lather. Rinse the coat well until you've gotten rid of all of the shampoo and then towel your dog dry. Some dogs may let you use the hairdryer on the low heat setting – my dog won't, so I have to spend a little extra time with the towel to make sure he is dry.

b. Trimming Your Havanese

Because the Havanese has such a long, thick coat, it is best to have it trimmed by a professional groomer. If you really want to trim your dog's coat at home, watch how the groomer does it a few times until you are sure that you can replicate the process. Even if you have your dog professionally groomed, you can still do some minor trimming of the hair on his feet and ears yourself. Trimming the hair between your dog's toes once a week will help to keep it from becoming matted. You might also want to trim the hair inside your dog's ears to help keep them dry and to prevent ear infections.

c. Clipping the Nails

Another grooming task you can probably handle yourself is trimming your dog's nails. Before you do it for the first time, however, it is a good idea to have your vet or groomer show you how. A dog's nail contains a blood vessel called the quick which provides the blood supply to the nail. If you cut your dog's nail too short you could sever the quick – this will not only be painful for your dog, but it will likely cause profuse bleeding as well. Your best bet is to trim the minimum amount of nail each time and to do it frequently enough that the nails don't become overgrown.

d. Cleaning the Ears

Dogs with floppy ears covered in hair tend to experience frequent ear infections because the inner ear doesn't get enough air circulation. If your dog's ears get wet, they become a breeding ground for bacteria, and that can lead to infection. To clean your dog's ears, squeeze a few drops of dog ear cleaner into the ear canal then massage the base of your dog's ear to distribute the solution. Use a clean cotton ball or swab to remove wax and debris as well as any excess solution then let your dog's ears air-dry.

Chapter Six: Havanese Dog Training Guide

With the right training, you can tame even the most energetic Havanese dog!

In addition to ensuring that your Havanese dog's basic needs are met, it is also your responsibility to train him. Havanese dogs are relatively intelligent, and they generally respond well to training. You will, however, need to dedicate a good bit of time to training your dog if you want him to become an obedient adult. In this chapter, you will receive an overview of some popular dog training methods so you can choose which method you want to use. I will also provide you with a recommendation for my favorite training method for Havanese dogs as well as some tips for crate training your dog.

1.) Overview of Dog Training Methods

If you do a little research, you will find that there are many different types of dog training methods out there. Each dog trainer puts his own unique twist on it, but the basics of certain training methods are largely the same. To help you understand the difference between dog training methods, I will group them into two categories: punishment-based and rewards-based. It all depends on the method you use to teach your dog what he is and is not allowed to do and to teach him to respond to your commands.

One of the dog training methods you will come across as you do your own research is the one used by Cesar Milan, the "Dog Whisperer". This approach is called Alpha Dog training, and it hinges on the idea that dogs are pack animals and, as the dog owner, it is your job to become the alpha male. In order to do so, you will need to make sure that your dog is submissive to you by establishing yourself as the dominant leader. You must never let your dog eat before you do or walk with the dog in front of you. You may also need to discipline your dog for undesired behavior to reduce their frequency.

While this method works for some people (especially for more stubborn or independent breeds), I don't personally recommend it for Havanese dogs because it will not help you foster the kind of relationship you want to have with your dog. The same applies for other punishment-based training methods – these methods require you to punish your dog for certain behaviors to reduce the chances that your dog will do them again. Unfortunately, unless you punish your dog in the act or immediately after, he is unlikely to connect the punishment with the crime. If you punish your dog too much, he could end up fearing you, and he may just be confused by the punishment.

The opposite of punishment-based training is rewards-based training. This type of training involves rewarding your dog for performing desired behaviors in order to encourage him to repeat them. The most popular type of rewards-based training is positive reinforcement training. With this type of training you use treats and/or praise to reward your dog for performing the desired behavior, encouraging him to repeat it in the future. Food is a very strong motivation for dogs which is why this training method is so highly effective.

Another variation of positive reinforcement training that you might try is called clicker training. With this type of training you use the same kind of training sequence as standard positive reinforcement training in which you reward the dog for performing the desired behavior. With clicker training, however, you add a step between the command the reward – at the instant your dog performs the behavior you want, you click the clicker and then immediately reward him. The clicker helps the dog to identify more quickly the behavior you are trying to reinforce. The key, however, is to use the clicker only for the first few repetitions until he identifies the behavior – then you phase it out, so he doesn't become dependent.

2.) Best Training Method for Havanese Breed

When it comes time for training be sure to have some tasty treats on hand!

My personal favorite training method for Havanese dogs is positive reinforcement training. Not only is this training method one of the most effective options out there, but it actually encourages your dog to form a positive bond with you during the process. The last thing you want to do is to accidentally have your dog associate you with a negative stimulus. You want your dog to WANT to listen to you, and positive reinforcement training is the best way to make sure that that happens.

The key to success with positive reinforcement training is consistency. You want to choose a simple command (like Sit or Stay) and then stick to it – make sure everyone in your family uses the same word for each command. You also need to be consistent about praising and rewarding your dog each and every time he performs the desired behavior on command. If you only reward him for following your commands two out of five times, your dog will become confused, and it will take longer to train him.

It is also important that you choose the right motivation for your dog during training. Food is usually the best motivation for dogs, but you need to be careful about giving your dog too many treats. Try to choose some very small treats that have a strong smell to attract your dog's attention. You can also try holding one of your daily training sessions around meal time so you can use the pieces of your dog's kibble as rewards. Some dogs are also motivated by physical rewards – a quick minute of playtime with a favorite toy or a tummy rub.

a. Sample Training Sequence

If you do it right, you can use positive reinforcement to teach your dog to do just about anything. When you first start training, however, it is a good idea to start with something simple like the Sit command. From there you can move on to other commands like Lie Down, Come, or Stay.

To teach your dog these commands, follow a training sequence like the one below:

1. Kneel down in front of your Havanese dog and hold a small treat between the thumb and forefinger of your dominant hand.

2. Get your dog's attention with the treat by waving it in front of his nose so he catches the smell.

3. Hold the treat just in front of your dog's nose and tell him to "Sit" in a firm and clear tone.

4. Immediately move the treat up and forward toward the back of your dog's head.

5. Your Havanese should lift his nose to follow the treat and, in doing so, his bottom will lower to the floor – if he doesn't respond this way, start over.

6. As soon as your dog's bottom hits the floor, tell him "Good dog" and give him the treat.

7. Repeat this training sequence several times until your Havanese responds consistently with the

appropriate behavior.

8. Continue practicing with your dog, slowly reducing the frequency of food rewards but remaining consistent with verbal praise.

If you follow this type of training sequence, and you are consistent about praising and rewarding your dog every time, it should only take a few repetitions until he starts to get the hang of it. Once your dog thoroughly understands the command you can start to phase out the food rewards, so he doesn't become dependent on them – just make sure to praise your dog every time.

3.) *Havanese Puppy Crate Training Guide*

In addition to teaching your Havanese dog basic obedience, you must also housebreak him. The method I recommend for housetraining is crate training. If you do it right, your dog will not come to view the crate as punishment – he should look at it as a special space to call his own, and he will go there for naps voluntarily. Once your Havanese is used to the crate you can start using it for crate training. Like any training method, crate training requires you to be firm and consistent in your rewards and praise – the more consistent you are, the faster he will learn.

Here is the training sequence I personally recommended for crate training a Havanese:

1. Choose a specific part of your backyard where you want your Havanese dog to do his business – you can fence off a small area or simply choose a particular corner.

2. Take your puppy outside every hour or two and lead him directly to this chosen location each and every time you take him out.

3. Tell your Havanese "Go pee" (or choose another simple command) as soon as he gets to that particular area.

4. Wait for your Havanese puppy to do his business – if he does, immediately praise him in a very excited voice and give him a small treat as a reward.

5. If your Havanese doesn't have to go, immediately take him back inside instead of letting him wander.

6. Keep a close eye on your Havanese at all times when he is in the house – try to confine him to whatever room you are in so you can watch him.

7. Watch your Havanese for signs that he has to go and take him outside immediately if he starts to sniff the ground, walk in circles, or squat – this is in addition to taking him out every hour or two.

8. When you cannot physically watch your Havanese, keep him confined to his crate to reduce the risk of him having an accident – do not keep any food or water in the crate with him.

9. Limit your dog's time in the crate to just a few hours until he is old enough to hold his bladder and bowels

for a longer period of time.

10. Always let your Havanese dog outside immediately before putting him in the crate and after releasing him – you should also take him out after a meal or after a nap.

Like any kind of positive reinforcement training, crate training requires you to be as consistent as possible. Just make sure that you give your puppy as many chances as you can to do his business outside – if you do, he will be much less likely to have an accident in the house. If you are firm and consistent, you can housebreak your Havanese dog in just a few weeks!

Chapter Seven: Havanese Dogs Breeding Guide

Look at this photogenic Havanese family! Don't you want one for yourself?

Breeding your Havanese dog is not something you should take on without careful consideration. Not only is raising a litter of puppies a big responsibility, but caring for a pregnant dog is as well; there are also many complications that could occur during whelping that could put your dog in danger. Before you decide whether to breed your dog or not, take the time to learn the basics about dog breeding as well as some specifics about breeding Havanese dogs – you will find all of this information and more in this chapter.

1.) *General Havanese Dog Breeding Information*

If your primary goal for breeding your Havanese dog is to make money selling the puppies, think again. It may come as a surprise for you to learn that most breeders are lucky to make any profit at all on breeding (they are lucky to break even). Between the cost of stud service for a well-bred male dog and the cost of caring for a pregnant dog, dog breeding is not an inexpensive endeavor. There is also a great deal of time and effort that goes into it to ensure that mother and puppies are in good health. The only reason you should breed your Havanese dog is out of a personal interest to preserve or improve the breed.

a. Precautions and Risks

Before you breed your Havanese dog, you need to be well aware of the potential risks involved. Breeding puts a lot of strain on a female dog's body, and it can be extra stressful for small-breed dogs like the Havanese to carry around that much extra weight. If you breed your Havanese too early, she could be too young to carry a litter to term or she could experience dangerous complications during the birth. The risks for male dogs that are associated with breeding are much lower, though there are still some potential problems that come with leaving a male dog intact instead of having him neutered as a puppy.

The Havanese Club of America, Inc. sets specific breeding guidelines and standards to ensure the safe and responsible breeding of Havanese dogs. In addition to stating that "every breeding [should] be done from the standpoint of bettering the breed," there are guidelines in terms of breeding age as well. Male dogs should not be used in breeding prior to 1 year of age, and they should not be used after 12 years of age. Females should not be bred prior to 18 months of age or after 8 years. Both males and females need to be in good health, free of any communicable disease, and free from genetic faults. They should also be examined by a veterinarian to rule out hereditary eye diseases.

In addition to following these general rules, you should also have your female Havanese thoroughly checked out by a veterinarian before breeding to ensure that she is healthy enough and mature enough to bear a litter. Feed your Havanese a healthy, nutritious diet to condition her for breeding as well. You won't have to change her diet drastically during the pregnancy, but you should be prepared to feed her a little bit more in the final stages to help her support her own body as well as the development of the puppies. Your vet will be able to help you determine the best diet for your pregnant Havanese.

b. Basic Dog Breeding Information

Now that you understand a little bit more about the thought and planning that goes into breeding Havanese dogs you may be curious to learn the details about dog breeding. While details vary a little bit from one breed to another, the basics of dog breeding are largely the same in most cases. When a female dog is mature enough for breeding, she will start to go through the estrus cycle, also known as "heat." In many cases, female dogs have their first heat around 6 months of age – this is why you should spay your dog before this age if you do not plan to breed her. It is important to note that while your Havanese dog's body may be physically capable of breeding at this age, it is not recommended that you breed her during her first heat cycle – wait until she is 18 months old.

The heat cycle for female dogs occurs twice a year in most cases, though some small-breed dogs will go into heat three times per year. The cycle lasts between 2 and 4 weeks with an average length of about 21 days. During the heat cycle, your dog's ovaries will release eggs and, if she is mated to an intact male dog during this period, conception will occur, and the dog will become pregnant. Some of the signs that indicate your dog is going into heat may include:

- Swelling of the external vulva

- Bloody discharge from the vaginal area
- Increased frequency of urination, urine marking behavior
- Vocalization, whining or howling

The swelling of the vulva is usually the first sign of heat in most dogs, though some develop a discharge first. The color and thickness of that discharge will change throughout the course of the heat cycle, and you can use it to tell what stage of the cycle your dog is in. At first, the discharge is usually fairly red and bloody, but it will become more watery and pink in color about 7 to 10 days into the cycle – this is the point at which your dog is most fertile so you should introduce her to the male dog at this point. Keep in mind, however, that sperm can survive in the female's reproductive tract for 5 to 7 days, so pregnancy can occur even days after mating.

If your female Havanese becomes pregnant, then she will go into something called the gestation period – this is the period of time during which the eggs developed into fetuses inside her uterus. The gestation period for most dogs lasts between 61 and 65 days, about 9 weeks, but the average length is 63 days. At the end of the gestation period, the dog will whelp the puppies (give birth), and she will care for them until they are old enough to become independent.

2.) Raising Havanese Puppies Information

Nothing says "love" like a smile from a newborn puppy!

While your Havanese dog is pregnant, you will need to keep a close eye on her to make sure she doesn't experience any complications. You need to feed her a high-quality, nutritious diet, but you generally will not need to increase the amount you feed her until later in the pregnancy. It is a good idea just to offer your Havanese dog as much food as she needs; she will stop eating when she has had enough. Your vet will be able to tell you whether she is gaining weight at a healthy rate or if you need to cut back on feeding her a little bit.

In order to predict when your Havanese will give birth, you need to keep track of her cycle. Again, the gestation period lasts anywhere from 61 to 65 days, so mark your calendar with the expected due date. Near the end of the gestation period, you will need to provide your dog with a safe place to whelp her puppies. A nice big box in a dark, quiet area is a good option. Just line it with newspaper and old towels that you don't mind getting dirty – you can throw them out and replace them after the birth.

As your Havanese dog approaches her due date, she will start spending more and more time in the whelping box. Try not to disturb her, but keep an eye on her so you will be able to tell when she starts going into labor. The best way to predict when the puppies will be born is to start taking her internal temperature within a few days of her due date. The average internal temperature for a dog is between 100°F to 102°F (37.7°C to 38.8°C). Once it drops to about 98°F (36.6°C), labor is likely to begin within the hour. You will know that labor is starting when your dog starts to show obvious signs of discomfort like pacing, panting, and changing positions.

When your Havanese dog starts to give birth, stay nearby but let her do it on her own. In the early stages of labor, contractors will occur about 10 minutes apart. If your Havanese has contractions for more than 2 hours without giving birth, take her to the emergency vet immediately.

When she does start giving birth, she will whelp one puppy about every half hour. After the puppy is born, she will tear open the birth sac and bite through the umbilical cord. She will then clean the puppy and lick him to stimulate his breathing before the next puppy is born.

After all of the puppies have been born, your Havanese will expel the afterbirth. You shouldn't be surprised if she eats it – it is rich in nutrients, and she needs some extra energy at this point. Make sure the puppies begin nursing within an hour of being born, so they get some of the colostrum. Colostrum is the first milk the mother produces, and it is full of nutrients and antibodies from the mother's immune system. The puppies will rely on these antibodies for protection until their own immune systems develop. If the puppies won't nurse, you may need to hand feed them to make sure they get the nutrition they need.

The average litter size for the Havanese dog breed is 1 to 9 puppies; this is fairly large, especially for a small-breed dog. In most cases, however, Havanese dogs have 4 or 5 puppies. When they are born, Havanese puppies generally weigh no more than 3 to 6 ounces (85 to 170g), though they will grow quickly over the coming weeks. Havanese puppies can be expected to gain 1 to 2 grams per day per pound of anticipated adult body weight. You should weigh the puppies on a daily basis for the first two weeks to ensure that they are growing properly, then you can cut back to weighing them just once a week. If the puppies lose weight, take them to the vet for a check-up – it is normal for puppies to lose up to 10% of their birth weight within the first 24 hours after birth, but they should start gaining weight after that point.

When they are born, Havanese puppies are blind, and they have a very limited amount of hair. They are completely dependent on their mother, and they will spend most of their time nursing and sleeping. The puppies will begin to crawl between 7 and 14 days, and they should be able to walk by 21 days. The teeth start to erupt between 2 and 4 weeks of age, and all of the teeth should have grown in by the time the puppies are 8 weeks old. Their ears will open around day 14, and they may start eating small amounts of softened solid food around 3 weeks of age.

By the time the puppies are 5 weeks old, they will be playing with each other, and their personalities will start to develop. Over the next two to three weeks the puppies should be given more soft food to encourage them to wean off their mother's milk. At 6 to 7 weeks they will start their puppy vaccinations and, by 8 weeks, they should be completely weaned. You can handle the puppies from a very young age, and it is recommended that you do so in order to socialize them. Once the puppies are weaned, they can be separated from their mother.

Chapter Eight: Havanese Dog Health Guide

Keep your Havanese dog's health on track with vaccinations and a healthy diet!

Once you bring your Havanese dog home, you will bond quickly, and he will become a member of the family. As such, you will want to do everything you can to keep him happy and healthy. In addition to providing your Havanese with a high-quality diet, you also need to make sure he has access to routine veterinary care – he needs at least one check-up a year, and he will need a number of shots. In this chapter, you will learn about potential health issues affecting the breed so you can spot them early if they happen to ensure that your dog gets prompt treatment.

1.) *Common Health Problems for Havanese Dogs*

The Havanese breed is very healthy in general and feeding your dog a high-quality diet will help to ensure his health and well-being for as long as possible. Still, there are certain inherited conditions as well as other health problems which have been known to affect the breed that you should be aware of. The more you know about the Havanese breed, the better you will be able to care for your own dog – this includes familiarizing yourself with common conditions known to affect the breed. If you learn about the common signs and symptoms of these health problems, you will know what to look for, and you can seek veterinary care for your dog at the first sign of trouble.

In this section, you will find an overview of some of the health conditions that may affect your Havanese so you will be prepared if your dog ever becomes ill. <u>Some of the conditions most commonly affecting the Havanese breed include the following</u>:

- Cataracts
- Chondrodysplasia
- Deafness
- Heart Disease
- Hip Dysplasia
- Legg-Calve-Perthes Disease

- Liver Shunt
- Patellar Luxation
- Progressive Retinal Atrophy
- Tear Staining

In the following pages, you will receive an overview of each of these conditions including their clinical signs and symptoms, methods of diagnosis, treatment options, and prognosis information.

a. Cataracts

For Havanese dogs, cataracts are usually an inherited condition – this is why DNA screening is so important for breeding, to prevent passing the disease on to other dogs. A cataract is an opacity that forms in the lens of the dog's eye which can obstruct his vision. Cataracts generally are not painful for dogs, but they can become large enough to obstruct the dog's vision completely, causing total blindness. There is also a risk that the cataract could luxate, or slip out of position and start to float around the eye – this can sometimes be painful for the dog, and it can block fluid drainage from the eye, causing glaucoma which can lead to permanent loss of vision.

Unfortunately, cataracts cannot be prevented, especially if it is an inherited condition for your dog. If the cataract is caught in the early stages, however, your vet may be able to do something to help preserve your dog's vision. In some cases, vision can be restored through surgery – this type of treatment generally has a very high success rate, though there is a fairly long recovery period. Cataracts can sometimes be correlated with a secondary condition – treating that condition is also essential for the treatment of cataracts themselves.

b. Chondrodysplasia

Chondrodysplasia is a term that refers to an abnormal growth of cartilage that can lead to disproportionate dwarfism. The Havanese is already a small dog which increases its risk for musculoskeletal problems, but genetic abnormalities like chondrodysplasia can further exacerbate these issues, leading to problems like limb shortening, teeth crowding, poor growth, enlarged joints, or bowing of the limbs. This is a genetically inherited condition, and it can be far-reaching – another good reason to ensure that your Havanese was properly bred from DNA-tested stock.

There are two different types of chondrodysplasia – osteochondrodysplasia and achondroplasia. The first category, osteochondrodysplasia, is a genetic abnormality that affects the bone and cartilage, causing bone deformities and inhibiting normal growth. Achondroplasia is a type of osteochondrodysplasia that causes the bones to grow to less than the normal size for the breed. This is the result of a mutation in the growth factor receptor gene. Chondrodysplasia in dogs is an autosomal dominant genetic disorder which means that only one parent needs to have the gene for the puppy to potentially develop the disease during its life.

Unfortunately, there is no definitive treatment for chondrodysplasia in dogs. After your veterinarian makes the diagnosis he may recommend surgery to repair any deformities but the results of these surgeries are often not rewarding. In many cases, the dog's lifespan will be shortened by the disease and the best treatment is to manage pain and inflammation with analgesics and anti-inflammatory medications. The prognosis for this condition varies depending on the severity.

c. Deafness

While any dog can develop deafness or a loss of hearing, it is often a congenital problem for the Havanese breed. It is possible to screen for this condition, but there is no treatment option if the dog has it. In some cases, Havanese puppies are born able to hear, and they lose their hearing over time – other puppies are born deaf. The signs that your dog is losing his hearing may include reduced responsiveness to its name, reduced response to commands and everyday sounds, failure to wake or respond to loud or startling noises.

Though it may take time for your dog to lose his hearing completely, it will be very easy for your vet to diagnose it. Deafness is one of the very few conditions that a vet can identify almost immediately upon walking into the exam room. Though there is likely nothing that can be done to stop or repair your dog's deafness, there is no reason why he cannot live a long and healthy life. You will need to make certain accommodations such as reducing your dog's activity and taking precautions to avoid injury, but he can still live an otherwise normal life.

d. Heart Disease

Cardiovascular disease is a relatively common health problem affecting dogs in general, but it seems to affect Havanese dogs to a higher degree than some other breeds. In dogs, heart disease can simply be the result of old age or it can be secondary to some kind of infection or another health problem. Certain dogs are born with heart defects and others develop heart problems as a result of poor diet and lack of exercise.

The signs of heart disease in dogs can be difficult to notice at first because some of them seem like normal things your dog occasionally does anyway, like coughing. If your dog starts coughing more than usual, however, or if it appears to happen more during or after exercise or a few hours before bed, it could be a sign of a problem. Tiring very easily or having breathing problems can also be signs of heart disease, as can pacing around bedtime and having trouble settling down.

If left untreated, heart disease can become very serious for Havanese dogs, so have your dog checked out at the first sign of a problem. Your vet may need to perform blood and urine tests as well as chest x-rays, an EKG, and an ultrasound. The treatment for heart disease will vary depending on the cause of the condition. In some cases, medications may be able to correct an abnormal heart rhythm or surgery might be required to correct a problem. Dietary changes and reducing your dog's activity level may help as well. Helping your dog maintain a healthy body weight will help to reduce any extra strain on his heart, so that will be part of his treatment as well.

e. Hip Dysplasia

This condition is related to the hip joint and its ability to keep the head of the femur (the leg bone) in place. Hip dysplasia is an inherited condition that usually involves an anatomical abnormality in the joint structure or a laxity of the muscles and connective tissues that help to keep the femoral head in place. Dogs with hip dysplasia occasionally have the femoral head pop out of the socket in the hip joint; the more often it happens, the more the bone becomes worn down, and the dog will develop osteoarthritis.

In many cases, dogs with hip dysplasia do not experience any pain during the early stages – in fact, they may not even show any signs or symptoms except for altered gait when the bone is out of place and pain or soreness after it pops back in. In very severe cases, puppies under 6 months of age may show signs of pain or discomfort during exercise and the condition can progress to the point that normal daily activities become painful.

Signs that your Havanese dog has hip dysplasia may include moving with an altered gait, reluctance to straighten the joint, stiffness or pain in the rear legs (especially in the morning or after exercise), difficulty climbing stairs, and limping. As the condition worsens, the dog may lose muscle tone and could have trouble getting up – he may even become lame in the affected limb. There are several surgical treatments available for hip dysplasia and medications can help to manage the pain and inflammation. Helping your dog maintain a healthy weight is crucial for managing this condition.

f. Legg-Calve-Perthes Disease

Similar to hip dysplasia, Legg-Calve-Perthes disease is a condition that affects the head of the femur bone. Whereas hip dysplasia involves the femoral head popping in and out of joint, however, this disease involves degeneration of the head which causes inflammation and osteoarthritis. Legg-Calve-Perthes disease does not have a known cause, but it commonly happens that dogs with the disease have blood supply issues to the femoral head. This disease is most commonly seen in small and miniature breeds, and it usually manifests between the ages of 5 and 8 months.

Some of the most common symptoms of Legg-Calve-Perthes disease include gradual onset of lameness, carrying of the affected limb, pain when moving the hip joint, and wasting of the thigh muscles. In order to diagnose your Havanese with the disease, your vet will need to have x-rays taken of the limb. In terms of treatment, surgical options are available to repair the joint and physical therapy is usually required to help rehabilitate the limb. Regular exercise is also a vital part of treatment – the dog needs to rebuild the muscle in the limb to restore normal function and movement.

g. Liver Shunt

A liver shunt is also known as a ductus venosus, and it is something that develops when puppies are still growing in their mother's uterus. While puppies are in the uterus, their livers are not functional, so the blood bypasses the liver through the shunt, and the mother's body detoxifies the blood for the puppy. When the puppies are born, the shunt is supposed to close, so the liver becomes functional – if it doesn't, the puppy has what is called an open shunt or patent ductus venosus. There is another type of shunt called an extra-hepatic liver shunt which is a type of genetic anomaly which results in the blood being rerouted around the liver by an abnormal blood vessel.

Some of the signs that your Havanese might have a liver shunt include poor growth, lethargy, drooling, increased thirst, walking in circles, and constipation – it can even lead to liver toxicosis. Symptoms of liver toxicosis may include vomiting, diarrhea, and even seizures. Fortunately, liver shunts can be surgically repaired to restore normal blood flow. Putting your dog on a restricted protein diet may also help, and certain medications are beneficial as well.

h. Patellar Luxation

The patella is bone on the front of the femur, also known as the kneecap. There is a groove in the femur bone which allows the patella to move up and down as the dog bends his knee. When the kneecap starts to move out of position, however, it is called patellar luxation. Patellar luxation in dogs can be the result of injury or trauma to the limb, but it is often the result of a genetic malformation. When the patella is out of position, the dog cannot straighten its knee until the quadriceps muscles relax and the patella slides back into place.

Patellar luxation is fairly common in small-breed dogs like the Havanese, especially in dogs with very short legs. Dogs with patellar luxation generally don't experience any pain except when the patella luxates, and they may have some soreness or stiffness after it slips back into place. The more frequently this starts to happen, the greater the chance that the dog will develop osteoarthritis in the joint. Fortunately, surgery is usually very effective in repairing the joint. In very mild cases, medical therapy is sufficient.

i. Progressive Retinal Atrophy

An inherited eye condition, progressive retinal atrophy
(PRA) affects the retina of the eye, the part that receives
light and transmits it to the brain where it is interpreted as
vision. There are several different forms of PRA in dogs like
the Havanese breed and they manifest at different ages. In
healthy dogs, the retina develops around 8 weeks of age;
dogs with PRA, however, usually exhibit arrested
development of the retina, or the photoreceptors start to
degenerate from an early age. Most dogs with PRA show
signs of degeneration by 2 months of age and most are
completely blind within one year.

Unfortunately, progressive retinal atrophy has no cure, and
no treatment can help to slow the progression of the disease
– that is why DNA screening is essential for Havanese dogs,
to make sure that this condition isn't passed on. Though
PRA cannot be cured, most dogs adapt well to the loss of
vision. You will have to make some accommodations and
avoid rearranging the furniture in your home, but your dog
can lead an otherwise normal life even with progressive
retinal atrophy. Just keep in mind that dogs with PRA
should not be bred – you should also notify the breeder of
your dog if he has the disease.

j. Tear Staining

In Havanese dogs, tear staining is not a disease, but it can sometimes be a sign of a problem. Sometimes a dog's eyes simply produce excessive tears and sometimes the hair around the dog's eyes causes irritation which makes the eye water, leading to stains in the corners of the eye. In some cases, however, the staining may be the result of blocked tear ducts; this is commonly the case in dogs with short faces like the Havanese. Fortunately, tear staining is generally not painful or dangerous for your dog; it is mostly an aesthetic problem.

If your Havanese dog develops tear stains, you should have him checked out by a veterinarian to make sure he doesn't have some kind of medical problem. In some cases, blocked tear ducts can be repaired through surgery or medications. It may also be the case that your dog's tear stains are caused by ingredients in his food or minerals in your tap water. Cleaning your dog's tear stains is relatively easy – just soak a cloth in warm water or sterile saline solution and gently clean the stains away. You can also try using a 3% hydrogen peroxide solution.

2.) *Havanese Dog Vaccinations and Precautions*

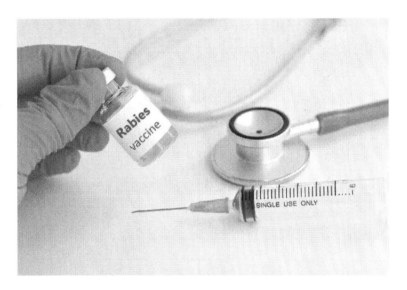

Ouch! Don't forget about routine vaccinations!

Familiarizing yourself with some of the most common conditions known to affect the Havanese breed will go a long way in helping to keep your dog healthy and happy. In addition to knowing what to look for and making sure that your Havanese sees the vet often enough, you should also ensure that he gets the vaccinations he needs. Vaccines help to protect dogs against certain contagious and deadly diseases like parvovirus, rabies (US only), and distemper. Your vet will be able to tell you exactly which vaccines your Havanese dog needs and when he needs them. He will need certain vaccines more frequently as a puppy, but once

he grows up, he will only need booster shots once a year –
some shots even come in 3- or 5-year versions.

To help you understand which vaccines your Havanese is
likely to need and when … consult this vaccination
schedule for dogs:

Vaccination Schedule for Dogs**			
Vaccine	Doses	Age	Booster
Rabies (US only)	1	12 weeks	annual
Distemper	3	6-16 weeks	3 years
Parvovirus	3	6-16 weeks	3 years
Adenovirus	3	6-16 weeks	3 years
Parainfluenza	3	6 weeks, 12-14 weeks	3 years
Bordetella	1	6 weeks	annual
Lyme Disease	2	9, 13-14 weeks	annual
Leptospirosis	2	12 and 16 weeks	annual
Canine Influenza	2	6-8, 8-12 weeks	annual

Chapter Nine: Havanese Dogs Showing Guide

If you can tame his fluffy coat, your Havanese will steal the show!

The Havanese is a very attractive dog breed, and it is very popular in the show circuit. It is important to realize, however, that not all Havanese dogs are of show-quality – there is a Havanese breed standard that your dog must adhere to if you want to show him. Showing your dog can be a lot of fun, but it can be challenging as well, especially keeping your dog's coat clean and in good show condition. In this chapter, you will learn about the Havanese breed standard set by the AKC and the UK Kennel Club as well as some general tips for showing dogs.

1.) *Havanese Dog Breed Standard*

Different breed clubs have specific standards for all of the breeds they accept for show. This breed standard dictates the ideal size and weight for the breed and provides details for conformation as well. Unless your Havanese is an excellent example of the breed standard, he will not do well in a dog show. Keep in mind that breed standards may vary slightly from one breed club to another – this is the case for the American Kennel Club and The Kennel Club in the United Kingdom. In this section, you will find an overview of the key points in the Havanese breed standard for both of these national dog clubs.

a. American Kennel Club Standard

General Appearance and Temperament

The Havanese dog is small and sturdy with a playful, spirited personality. The breed is friendly and intelligent, having a unique springy gait and a long, untrimmed, double coat. The dog can be shown either brushed or corded with no hair accessories.

Head and Face

The head is broad and slightly rounded, the muzzle full and rectangular with a broad, dark nose (black, except in chocolate dogs). The eyes are large and dark brown with a soft but intelligent expression. The ears are dropped, broad at the base with a distinct fold.

Body and Tail

The body is slightly longer than the height measured at the withers with well-sprung ribs and a short, well-muscled loin and a moderate tuck. The neck is slightly arched, blending into the shoulders. The chest is deep and the topline straight, rising slightly from withers to croup. The tail is high-set and carried forward over the back. It is well plumed with long, silky hair.

Legs and Feet

The upper arm is short, and the elbows are carried close to the body. The forelegs are straight, the pasterns short and strong. The hind legs are muscular with moderate angulation. The feet have high arched toes with pads and nails of any color.

Coat and Color

The coat is silky and light in texture, both for the undercoat and outer coat. The coat should be long and abundant with a wavy texture, standing slightly off the body and flowing with movement. The natural lines of the dog can be seen, and the coat may be corded. All colors and markings are permissible and of equal merit.

Size

The ideal height for the breed is 9 to 10 ½ inches, but the acceptable range is 8 ½ to 11 ½ inches. The dog should be moderately boned, not coarse or fragile.

Gait

The gait is springy, resulting from a short upper arm and powerful rear drive. The head is carried high with the slightly sloping topline holds while under movement.

Dogs that do not meet the minimum height requirement of 8 ½ inches and dogs that exceed 11 ½ inches (29cm) will be disqualified. Other disqualifications include incomplete or lack of pigment in the rimming around the eye, lack of pigmentation in the nose, and color other than brown or black in the eyes, nose, and lips. A coarse, wiry coat and a short, smooth coat will also be disqualified.

b. The Kennel Club Breed Standard

General Appearance and Temperament

The Havanese is a small, sturdy dog with a profuse coat and a plumed tail carried over the back. The breed is lively, affectionate, and intelligent with a friendly and outgoing temperament.

Head and Face

The skull is broad and slightly rounded with a moderate stop. The muzzle is not blunt, and the nose and lips are both solid black – in brown shades they may be brown. The eyes are large, dark, and almond shaped with black eye rims except in brown shades which may have lighter eyes with brown eye rims. The ears are dropped and moderately pointed, slightly raised and set just above eye level.

Body and Tail

The body is equal in height from elbow to ground and from withers to elbow. The dog is slightly longer from shoulder to buttock than the height at the withers. The tail is set high and carried over the back – it is profusely feathered with long, silky fur.

Legs and Feet

The hindquarters are medium boned with moderate angulation. The forequarters are medium boned, the legs straight and the shoulders well laid. The feet are small and tight with hare foot.

Coat and Color

The coat is soft and silky, wavy or slightly curled. The coat is full with an undercoat, and any color or combination of colors is considered permissible.

Size

The ideal size for the Havanese breed is 9 to 11 inches (23 to 28 cm) tall at the withers.

Gait

The gait is free with a springy step – the legs move parallel to the line of travel.

Any Havanese that departs from the points summarized above will be issued a fault – the seriousness of which will be determined in proportion to its degree and to its effect on the health and welfare of the dog as well as its impact on the dog's ability to perform its work.

2.) Tips for Showing Havanese Dogs

This Havanese is just begging for a medal!

There is a lot of detail and preparation that goes into showing your Havanese dog so make sure that you are up to the challenge before you decide to do it. Not only do you need to maintain your Havanese dog's coat at its full length, but you also have to train your dog for presentation. To show a dog, there are a few minimum requirements you need to adhere to in addition to the specific rules and regulations for the show.

On the next page you will find a list of some general requirements your dog should meet:

- The dog should be at least 12 months old – some shows have a puppy class, but not always.
- Make sure that your Havanese is completely housetrained and able to hold his bladder and bowels for at least 6 hours.
- Your dog should be an excellent example of the breed standard – no points of disqualification should be present.
- The dog should be properly socialized and able to handle being in a loud, crowded setting for extended periods of time.
- Your dog needs to have basic obedience training – he needs to respond to your commands and be able to behave in public.
- The dog needs to be up to date on all of his vaccinations – if your dog isn't vaccinated, there is a very real risk that he could contract a disease from another dog at the show.
- Your Havanese's coat needs to be completely natural and untrimmed except for minor trimming on the feet and genital region for cleanliness.
- Make sure that your dog's coat has been cleaned properly before the show and that it is entirely dry and brushed out, free from tangles and mats.
- Ensure that dog's coat appears natural (if not corded) – it should not be parted down the center of the back.

If your Havanese adheres to these basic requirements, you can move on to considering the rules and regulations of the specific show you plan to enter. Be sure to read the requirements very carefully and submit your registration on time. Always bring a copy of your registration to the show with you as well as some other basic supplies.

<u>Below you will find a list of some useful things you may need at the show</u>:

- Registration information
- Your dog's identification including license number and rabies vaccination info (US only)
- A dog crate and/or exercise pen
- A grooming table and any necessary grooming supplies or equipment
- Food, water, and treats for the entire day (for both you and your dog)
- Bowls for your dog's food and water
- Toys to keep your dog occupied
- Any medications your dog may need
- Paper towels, plastic gloves, and trash bags for after-show cleanup
- A change of clothes, just in case

In addition to being physically prepared for the show, you should also mentally prepare yourself. A dog show can be stressful for both you and your dog – it can also be very mentally draining because there is a lot of time spent waiting. You should also be realistic and not get your hopes up too high for your first couple of shows – it will take some time to become familiar with how things work in the show circuit and you should not expect your dog to be a winner right out of the gate.

When you are at the show, take advantage of the opportunity to network with fellow dog lovers. Don't be afraid to talk to the competition! You can learn a lot from other Havanese owners at the show, so don't hesitate to ask questions or to observe how experienced dog showers do things. The more you learn, the better you and your dog will get and the more likely you will be to win!

Chapter Ten: Havanese Dog Care Sheet

Don't let his innocent face fool you; Havanese puppies are quite the handful!

After reading this book, you should have a firm understanding of what the dog Havanese is like in general as well as what it is like as a pet. With this information in mind, it is my hope that you've decided that the Havanese is the right breed for you! If you are ready to join me as part of the Havanese fan club, you'll be glad to have this book as a resource once you bring your dog home. I realize, however, that you won't always have time to flip through the pages to find answers to your questions. This care sheet is here for your convenience, and it includes all of the basic facts and Havanese information you want to know.

1.) *Havanese Information Overview*

Pedigree: Bichon-type dog, may have been developed from the now-extinct Tenerife dog

AKC Group: Toy Group

Breed Size: small

Height: 8 to 12 inches (20 to 30.5 cm)

Weight: 7 to 13 pounds (3 to 6 kg)

Coat Length: very long

Coat Texture: soft and silky, often wavy; undercoat may or may not be present; outer coat is soft and light

Color: white, cream, tan, fawn, red, chocolate, brown, beige, black, silver, blue, etc.

Eyes and Nose: dark brown or black

Ears: flopped ears, well covered in fur

Tail: carried high over the back, feathered fur falls down onto the body

Temperament: friendly, lively, people-oriented, active

Strangers: may be shy around strangers but warms up quickly once introduced

Other Dogs: generally good with other dogs

Other Pets: generally, gets along with other pets

Training: intelligent and very trainable; may take longer to housetrain than larger dogs

Exercise Needs: not overly active or energetic; happy to spend most of its time inside with people

Health Conditions: heart disease, eye problems, tear staining, and some musculoskeletal issues like patellar luxation and hip dysplasia

Lifespan: average 14 to 16 years

2.) *Havanese Habitat Information Overview*

Space Requirements: does well in apartments and condos, does not need a great deal of space

Energy Level: moderate

Attention Needs: very people-oriented, should not be left alone for long periods of time

Exercise Requirements: average but not excessive, a daily walk plus active playtime will be sufficient

Crate: highly recommended; line with a comfy blanket or plush dog bed

Crate Size: just large enough to stand up, sit down, turn around, and lie down in comfortably

Toys: provide an assortment; be sure to include chew toys as well as interactive toys

Confinement: use a puppy playpen or a small spare room to provide your puppy with some personal space

Food/Water Bowls: place them in your puppy's area; stainless steel is the best material

Shedding Level: low

Brushing: at least several times a week; use a wire-pin brush and work through tangles with a comb

Trimming (Show): only allowed on the feet and in the genital region

Trimming (Pet): puppy clip or pet clip recommended for easy maintenance

Grooming Frequency: recommended every 6 to 8 weeks

Bathing: no more than every two weeks; bathing too frequently can dry out the dog's skin

Cleaning Ears: as needed, check at least once a week; use dog-friendly ear cleaning solution and cotton balls

Trimming Nails: once a week; trim the minimal amount needed to prevent overgrowth

3.) Havanese Nutritional Information Overview

Diet Type: carnivorous; derives nutrition from animal sources

Primary Nutrients: protein, fat, carbohydrates, water, vitamins, and minerals

Protein: made up of amino acids, supports growth and development of muscle and tissue

Amino Acids: total of 22, 10 of which are essential (need to come from the diet)

Fat: most concentrated source of energy; best from animal sources like chicken fat and fish oil

Carbohydrate: amount should be limited; best from digestible sources like whole grains (brown rice and oatmeal) or gluten-free sources (potatoes, peas, sweet potatoes)

Minimum Requirements (Puppy): 22% protein, 8% fat

Minimum Requirements (Adult): 18% protein, 5% fat

Ideal Range (Puppy): 22% to 32% protein, 10% to 25% fat

Ideal Range (Adult): 30% protein, up to 20% fat

Dog Food Points of Comparison: AAFCO statement of nutritional adequacy, guaranteed analysis, ingredients list

Recommended Proteins: fresh meats, poultry, eggs, seafood, meat meals

Recommended Fat: animal fat and fish oils

Nutrients: best from natural sources rather than synthetic supplements

Beneficial Additives: dried fermentation products, chelated minerals, vitamin supplements

Ingredients to Avoid: corn, wheat, and soy; artificial colors, flavors, and preservatives

Calorie Needs: 300 to 500 calories daily, varies by size, age, and activity level; average 41 calories per pound bodyweight

Meals per Day: two or three

Feeding Tips: choose a formula designed for small-breed dogs; feed several small meals

4.) Havanese Breeding Information Overview

Age of First Heat: around 6 months (or earlier)

Breeding Age (male): no younger than 1 year, no older than 12 years

Breeding Age (female): no younger than 18 months, no older than 8 years

Heat (Estrus) Cycle: 14 to 21 days

Frequency: twice a year, every 6 to 7 months; some small breeds have 3 cycles per year

Greatest Fertility: 7 to 10 days into the cycle

Gestation Period: average 63 days

Pregnancy Detection: possible after 21 days, best to wait 28 days before exam

Feeding Pregnant Dogs: maintain normal diet until week 5 or 6 then slightly increase rations

Signs of Labor: body temperature drops below normal 100° to 102°F (37.7° to 38.8°C), may be as low as 98°F (36.6°C); dog begins nesting in a dark, quiet place

Contractions: period of 10 minutes in waves of 3 to 5 followed by a period of rest

Whelping: puppies are born in 1/2 hour increments following 10 to 30 minutes of forceful straining

Puppies: born with eyes and ears closed; completely dependent on mother; sleep and nurse all day

Puppy Birthweight: 3 to 6 ounces (85 to 170g)

Puppy Development: crawling day 7 to 14; walking by day 21; sampling solid food at week 3, weaned by week 8

Litter Size: 1 to 9 puppies, 4 to 5 average

Weaning: start offering puppy food soaked in water at 5 to 6 weeks; fully weaned by 8 weeks

Socialization: start as early as possible to prevent puppies from being nervous as an adult

Conclusion

So, now that you've learned all that there is to know about the Havanese breed, what do you think? I hope and pray that you have come to love this breed as much as I do, and if you take the leap to bring home your own Havanese puppy I can confidently say that you won't be disappointed! It is my humble opinion that there is no better dog breed out there than the Havanese. Not only are they beautiful dogs with bright, shiny personalities but they are smart, playful and easy to train as well! That's the complete package if you ask me!

Before you dive into Havanese ownership, however, I want to mention one more thing – becoming a dog owner is more than just a choice. It is a responsibility! Your Havanese dog can be expected to live well over ten years, and it will be your job to love him and care for him throughout his entire life. As much as I might joke about my own Havanese, Bailey, being my favorite accessory. The truth is that he is part of the family. Dogs are more than just pets – they are friends and devoted companions, and they should be treated as such!

So, if you are ready to devote your life to becoming the best Havanese dog owner you can be, I hope you will follow in my footsteps and put all of the important information in this book to use. Good luck and God bless!

Index

C

D

E

F

G

H

I

R

S

T

U

V

W

Made in the USA
Las Vegas, NV
14 August 2022